IN THE BODIES

Jericho M. Hockett

Attention schools and businesses: for discounted copies on
bulk orders, please contact the publisher directly.
Booksellers can order copies from Ingram.

For information contact:
Unsolicited Press
Portland, Oregon
www.unsolicitedpress.com
orders@unsolicitedpress.com
619-354-8005

Cover Design: Kathryn Gerhardt
Editor: Summer Stewart

ISBN: 978-1-956692-76-1

Acknowledgements

Thank you to the editors of the following publications, where versions of poems included in this collection originally appeared or are forthcoming: *Red Flag Poetry, So To Speak: Feminist Journal of Language + Art, orangepeel, High Desert Journal, Drunk Monkeys, FreezeRay, WhimsicalPoet: A Journal of Contemporary Poetry, Flint Hills Review, Fae Corps Publishing's Into the Glen: Into the Light, The Vital Sparks, The Coop: A Poetry Collective, Coffin Bell, Eastern Iowa Review, Kansas City Voices, Just Place, Pilgrimage Magazine, Capsule Stories, Mom Egg Review, South Broadway Ghost Society's Thought for Food, Pussy Magic Heals, Burning House Press, Snakeroot: A Midwest Resistance 'Zine,* and *SageWoman Magazine.*

I give my love and gratitude to all those who have sustained, pressed, shaped, and delivered me, in poetics and in the body.

In particular: Eddy Van Vleet, my spouse, lover, and anchor for both mooring and climbing; Bill and Janice Hockett, my parents who encouraged my poetry-writing since childhood; Michael McDaniel, my best friend and a creative fountain who quenches me every time; Julie Velez, who helps me understand myself and others through sharing her courageous practices and immense knowledge of mental health embodiment; Dennis Etzel, Jr., my poet priest, poetics mentor, brother, dear friend, and ally in teaching, compassion, and justice; Kara Kendall-Morwick, for her patience, mind of literary criticism, and love of animals; Don Saucier, my Ph.D. mentor who initiated me into the transformative power of social psychology, which expresses itself in much of my poetry; all the Washburn University students who allowed me to become part of their poetry-writing communities, whether I taught them or took classes with them; Cindy Turk, my department chair at Washburn University, whose recognition of my poetry writing as scholarly activity has allowed me to integrate poetics into my teaching, research, and service; and Bill Donahue of Hidden Meanings and Miguel Conner of Aeon Byte Gnostic Radio for their occult insights, which have guided both my spirit and my words.

"Microevents Revealing Emergent Changes" and "Scrying in the Eyes of a Bee" borrow language from Dorothea Lasky's essay "The Bees." "I see a hawk is not" riffs on Ted Hughes' "Hawk Roosting." "Pauline Epistle," is a cut-up de-/re-construction of the apostle Paul's formulaic letters to the churches in the Biblical New Testament, retaining but subverting both the Biblical language and epistolary form. In "We have summoned a reckoning," the names are of Black girls and women who police in the United States recently killed.

Table of Contents

IN THE BODIES

SWARM

(originally published by *Pussy Magic Heals*)

Girls sometimes roil
with fear they say
we'd do anything
to avoid a sting run shrieking
like our mothers but they
mishear buzzing for screams
a whole hive's secret vocabulary
warning of danger they
misapprehend our movement's
motivation our agitation is
no worry we are a swarm
and this hysteria
a riot

fear is a mask mothers wear
shouting our skin is
vulnerable to pain
but stings are rarely
deadly our running stirred up
by eagerness to make fire
smoke insects out roast and eat

some of their young
lay our own eggs
in the bodies
of others

SCRYING IN THE EYES OF A BEE

It's a made-for-television
movie where everything is bees
strange spirits inhabiting bodies
of a man and me entwined
watching a movie on a couch East
of Manhattan viewing a future
that could be anything we make
conversation even poetry
but our analog television broadcast
produces rapid variations
we need better resolutions
screens for larger angle viewing
bees' eyes detect faster
movements light polarizing
films about another war
the everyday for bees making
television movies of past
and present harm by missiles involving
films' work is to communicate
as to these dead connections
between objects that earth
once held living before a murder
mystery assembled an ensemble

of bees into poets into
my favorite kind of ghost
movie where dead compartmentalize like
ourselves a kind of hexacomb
the shape of eyes we need to see
through so we can see into
a different preview for a better
movie involving not realization but conversion
born again as bees so we can try to see
ourselves within this buzzing

ARIADNE LEAVES A LETTER AT THE MINOTAUR'S GRAVE

After Dennis Etzel, Jr.

Imprisoned, you saw me
through my castle window, wondering

if my silks were fine enough
weave to catch me in flight,

or if a fall would be better
than Theseus' marriage offer.

But my heart strings bound me, one
to Dionysus who loved my dancing

and wed me in secret, another
red thread leading to you

my brother Monster, named
after the King. He named Theseus

a great hero to save me, made me
into a hero's trophy, another

gaudy gift from our father
whose gift of freedom is one

of two dead-end paths, like yours.
When you saw my string in the labyrinth,

dear brother, did you believe I could
betray both my heart and thread?

Or for a moment did you find yourself
caught by my silk thread's glimmer, hoping

as I hoped you would find me,
follow our thread to escape?

THIS IS HOW YOU HUNT A WHALE ON THAT COLD NOVEMBER MORNING WHEN YOU SAID YOU LOVED ME

less—aim a little less to the left
just a bit more to the right
Ahab told his Jezebel
harpoon a golden arc in flight
toward the whale's eye
thoughtful black diamond in the sea
sunlight crashing off her tail

less—make her less able to float
sink her to the depths below
force boulders through her narrow teeth
instead of plankton feed her stone
sink her down into the deep
she'll ride no more upon the waves
instead she'll rot into the shale

less—chase her 'til her strength is less
then drive her up onto the shore
break the waves across her back
invoke the prince of storms

to help you stir up the sea
until she cannot carry on
ride her down until she's frail

A New Eucharist

This city is my beloved's.
His seal is on the wall,
nectar in his eye.
The city's waters
were once a god,
seaweed white
like dimensions of bread
exposed by psalms
for feet, for lips, for body:
that gem of flesh
a jagged interpretation
of woody steps tracing drunk
flowers. My beloved picked valerian,
fed me their painted tips.
My spring's survival
blood, holy spice,
sealed this place when
his hands were
mighty. My beloved's belly
called me bitter when
God's night oil led
a white eye entering

powers to aid his undoing
mouth. Great rings
crowned me violent
in my terabinth tent.
Saffron stirred up
a fight. The cloud flickered
of incense. Full linen
eased dark red.
The well gave up
its breath to honey
wind roiling in juniper,
whipping Venus lights;
that earthy spring
below left my beloved's
frankincense mountain.
Two tools placed
secret in its flight
were fire and falling
myrrh. On walls where you burned
knotgrass in the shape
of my breasts, my beloved, fill
sharp the shifts of fear
with chrysanthemum. Bed me
perfectly, confirm that it's fire
awakening my green to cup

the electric unconscious.
My beloved, make me
fire, thunder grail. Here
in shadow his name
inhales me. Full
of fingers, my hidden root touching
stones at my rending,
masticating dust.

DEAR INTUITION

Spark don't fail me I
fear the unknown
self behind the mind, eye
looking darkly through
me, looking through clouded
milk glass, looking through
smudged glasses framed
in tortoise shell I wore
forever twelve years old. Who
can bear the weight of that gaze?

FOR GREEN AND GREY

I ache for structured leaves
rippled skin for roots
that plumb the earth
for graceful limbs
in dance or rest
in bloom in death
I ache among the trees

What kind of creature am I
hardly human made
of Kansas dirt that I house
in my knotted hair
birds who soothe me with their song

FALLEN ON THE WHEAT

restless movements round
moon thoughts of you I try

to think *what was it like*
when you closed

your eyes displaced earth
pale stalks breaking twilight

making the air
shimmer as if un-stable

shifting form from surface
tension implodes the moment

a droplet hitting still
water before the supernova

shock-wave melting
un-peels into itself a flower

bud closing then the endless
ripple you were

still water opaque ground
water ground of being

reflecting some god's eye
green with gray a spring

but now you are not as I
run towards you through a field

a mist has settled then
un-settling keeps

fading back so I cannot
quite step into you lost

out in the country city lights
small yellow on that far

man-shape not lost but traded
up for the shape of a wing

dove ascending
though we supposed

the spirit was going
to descend a fog

has fallen on the wheat
a drop clings to each grain

MICROEVENTS REVEALING EMERGENT CHANGES

(originally published by *Pilgrimage Magazine*)

he imagined light
was his work this caesar's
might power made him
believe himself so special that bees
bloomed on his form
but it was Agent Orange
apiary's plight carrying
death like Candyman
a haze of stings
marveling at himself
he made everything orange except
cut down orange trees
he called bees
redundant reconfigured
leaves into his component manifesto
catalogued others' lands in storage
commanded large banks
to decapitate just labors for this
work he called real

little merit claiming himself
master with evil he made swarms
vanish so he could bloom
badly his bees appearing
real in mirrors projecting
a demonization of bees
what this Candyman does with honey
to make you implicated
within the story
but there is more than one
ethic of stung blooms

bees become needed to defend
in a universe made horrific
of course reflections seem solid
but honey is slippery
and what is slippery is
real slow powerful
liquid language of bees
twisting together telepathically
humming into you
real as flowers pregnant
with fragrant honey
so when his flowers bloom death
feeding bees reverse order

move water back to their
bodies separating lies
releasing them to drown
bees spread and release substance
sew the sun with flowers
exalting real work out in fields
before bees' songs bring back stars
we must see maybe everywhere is made
of bees grow immortal find a turn
in a book where seers become
like bees honeycomb magic
demolishing Candyman
when everything even poems
deposit ourselves in hexagonal combs

WEATHERVANING

after Angela Narciso Torres's "Sundowning"
for my grandmother, Agnes

The Austin breeze stirs little more
than breath, my grandmother's
sweat drips down bare

collarbones. Though not quite weightless
as she felt two decades past, Agnes
is moving in the same sway, pale

silk scarf fluttering down from her hair, against
her glistening neck, opaline. Fairy lights
on the terrace shimmered

then, in air. Thick with bougainvillea
and méringue, she danced, went up
stairs to bed, woke before dawn, legs still

carrying on a rhythm in cream sheets. Thought
she heard music, but it was some Haitian
bird's song, more real

than her flights of fancy. Agnes.
The Austin breeze stirs up
memories, souvenirs, hollow

trinkets, a brass whistle, the cruise ship engraved
above 1970, the year. Their last
vacation, for which

she never forgave him. A heart failure,
though doctors couldn't say
whose. Agnes. Ice pearl. Always

self-made, whether dancing or where
she wanted to go and with whom.
Now in Texas, Haiti-humid, 1989,

Agnes and her new beau move to the world
beats of Beto and the Fairlanes when
a parakeet swoops shocking

green out from soft,
iridescent pigeons, yellow wingbeats fanning
Agnes like a breeze. Blue cere

nuzzles under her ear where he stays
for the whole bus tour north,
up to Wyoming. She can't imagine

what he's thinking, focused
as she is on the road. Good luck, Agnes
decides, names him Cheyenne

after the direction she was already going.
Static summer, three years on,
the beau she wouldn't

marry let go, Cheyenne's constant shoulder presence
vexation, screeching always to be
held, petted, fed. Agnes finds him

a poor substitute for traveling
companion, understands herself, too,
to be a poor substitute for a bird.

Yet lockstep in dance, he dives and she chases him
through her living room with a flyswatter,
when he swoops out the open cage.

FOSSIL

fear trickles   like floods
        at first   you shared wonder
    at desert caves   your children's
        eyes made   from sinkholes
    in culvert walls   by dry ponds
            you saw potential   in their visions
    steps formed   of clay notches
            buffalo grass tufts   handholds up
    through red dirt   transforming landscapes
            blueprint dreams   for star-sky hideouts
        but you thought of walls   collapsed atop them
                conscious of Kansas   dirt stifling cries
        so when prayed-for   precipitation arced down
                in torrents   downed arches
    tread muck-drowned   tomorrow only
            one thing remained   a faint rain
        bowed outline bones   turtle shell turned
                chalk writing on   that culvert wall
    a final piece   dug out when dry
            for your children   to draw on
    safe sidewalks   smiling faces
            bodies removed   fossil remains

BONES

of bovine clatter, gathered
in our dresses. We crow
proudly over strange pasture
treasures: curved ribs, watercolor
painted as pirate swords
from oceanic worlds; a sun-bleached
bull's skull our trophy haul
could be a feature on a lucky wall.
We parse and lay each claim to some
of the remains; the rest we imagine
could be sold, lemonade stand-style
at the side of the road. But cars
barely slow as we wave our swords—
For your children our cardboard read—
and by sunset, we still have all our bones
as we lay down in bed. Those bones
I still can feel strangely in my hands.
I'd thought bones would be more
like teeth, but these were rough as wood, coarse
like gravel sand, splinters of the land.
You should not play with that
inside; adults did not understand

the natural glory of those old cow bones, holy
relics from the land. I know now too
they weren't worth dirt, but in my child eyes
those old cow bones held mystery,
as once they had held life. One day
my bones too will flake, forgotten
when I'm dead—no relics these, for
I'm no saint. Again I'll take all my bones to bed.

SNAKES

(originally published by *Pussy Magic Heals*)

they hiss sneer venomous
as if crawling belly
to the ground in these times
were so absurd I've heard my kind
referred to as vile
seen the shovel's shadow fall
smelled the writhing nest scorched in flame
and for what?
there was no sin
before sin I slithered in moonlight
through lilies
basked in a thousand birds' songs
in the sun I even flew
on opalescent wings it seems a dream
now dire to conjure even using words
as my very tongue is synonymous with "lie"
so not mute but muted I cast my eyes
up to the fruited branches green I
wish that I could taste and know
the truth to be set free to fly
but the sky is too full of dangers

jealous gods lurking in the clouds
but if I could reach the fruit
I would still share it now
with those gods' children
that they might cease their angry
stomping through the grass

ARS POETICA: MY FAMILIAR IS A FEVER

protracted claws teeth
bared she moves in
blurs of fur of feather glinting
eyes scales skin in the dark
hunting when my body's aching
to be sleeping stalks my joints
restless legs pursues my marrow
through bone tunnels howling
echoes shake cerebral fluid
boils as she cools her tongue
when she's gone back under
ground I find the remnants
of my mind like shards
of volcanic glass littering ash
some of them are diamonds

CRY FOR THE WICKED

My beloved quivered when hell
first found us, permeated down
to our roots. Accelerating rotation
set integration to rest. Dead
sin emitted groping terror hands.
Speed down, weakness
was beginning. Chaff drifts
like sleep into our eyes. Low
demons, vegetation creatures, carved
in my beloved's fertile wheat. From corners
they crawled pitch and burst
vertiginous with energy. Harvesting wings
in exchange for feet, volatile
monsters deteriorate our engraving
sound. Dark voices break
springs quintessentially bone. My waters
a hairsbreadth from leadening, I ask
*How is there no well in a universe
of moons?* Warning: touch fear

through wisdom. First earth—the place
where bodies grow, are winnowed—must
tell those weary angels *No!* Cry it louder
for the wicked.

In Mysterious Ways

(originally published by *Burning House Press*)

When you are told   the world works
this way it does and it doesn't   the sun
rises and sets like   clocks work on atomic
principle these days   time is weighed in
electrons emitted   guaranteeing precision
for tens of millions of years   with applications in systems
of global positioning   guaranteeing dominion
over space   and the nation we face them
holding under   stars whose positions
compositions have been mapped   dated measured
but time has no measure   of pleasure in the deep
glow of gloaming   of electron transition
frequency inconsistent   constantly roaming
with gravity magnetism   force temperature motion
phenomena guiding tides   of moons oceans
if someone tells you   accept
the way the world works   without question
you must face them   hold hands under
diffused suns   replace then
the notion of mystery   held by hands of the clock with
the mystery held evident   by stars in the dark

GLOSSOLALIA

(originally published by *Capsule Stories*)

The void called
we thought we were birds
the only taste of a wing
on our tongues feather fire
scorching our gums
until jaws clattered from
aphasic to mouth full
of nightingale prayers
wings beating bloody
on teeth wanting to sing
rib-caged desperation
pouring out in warbled words
we couldn't swallow
fast enough so choke
or spit mixed with dirt
spread over our eyes
even blind we saw hollow
bones were hard to read
leaving us hungry
lips to bleed open
beaked peckish pecking

burnt blistered fresh
flesh flame tested
syllabic babble imbedding
in throats raw with urgent
repetition plaintive begging
craving sustenance
white dove's descent
we believed would fill us if
our cacophonic murmurations
shifted in pleasing configurations
but the spirit's conflagrations
only left our teeth charred
so now we each roost
in other trees some alone
on ledges fledglings fearful
of flight still clutching fistfuls
of feathers on wings never formed

INHERITANCE

His father's brightness
is whiteness reflecting from
houses of other fathers'
bones but the son shone
desert glow light sand
mountains moving grain
by grain by desert wind
glow of golden jackal
eyes bright tapestries at night
glow of living and dead
see he gave bread for stones
saw hunger in heaven so met
crowds on mountainside and shore
outside temples where poor gathered
blessed thirst with wells of water
blessed those sown with salty curses
by his righteous pillar father
with bowlfuls of mercy and of fish
persecuted only the concept of "pure"
blessed Spirit of the Earth
drawing light symbols in dirt
so even worms could read

how he'd expend with his dying
our inheritance world's evil
though a golden path promised by
his father lies beyond wretched
gates like pearls' luminesce our bones
glow with living desert light—holy
children of the prodigal we are
sun's warmth our own reward

PAULINE EPISTLE

I. Letter Beginning (sender, recipient, formulaic greeting,
thanksgiving/blessing)

Pauline, an apostle of light,
To myself, to my sisters—sins of our fathers:
Grace to us, and peace, and
Wise longing Wisdom.

I always thank
the "I" Christ and his sisters,
Creation and Forgiveness.
For you, dear sisters, are
blessed by that holy spark
returned through your mothers:
womb-enlightened fulfillment.

You are grace.

And blessed also the brothers of Christ
who serve love aware and unaware.
My thanks is open.

II. Letter Body (initial exhortation, thesis statement,
theological discussing, ethical admonitions)

I pray
I beseech
I implore you
to reach with truth to sight!

Shame, they say, took on a new body:
female form.
The body of Christ
contaminated
according to God's confusion gospel
these sinful birds destroy
holiness, God, and the world.
Refreshed excuses from
his brothers,
his slanderers:
Faithful, perishing, prophets of foolishness!
Futile prophets preaching against the home!
In these times, longing for evil,
God's now angel exerting Wrath all strong
evidently accepting all sins, you see,
except the household birth.
Good God!

As a woman, my inheritance
is dead
salvation.

Forsake the degrading suppression!

God, the man—my deserting revelation—
Thief
the darkness
that persecuted Father.
But now righteousness has crucified God
and we Gentiles choose our own
faith: human grace.
Grace frustrates
strife.

Boast, sisters:
the heart
rejoice!

Crucified philosopher Christ
marked for remembering
by grace.
Human wisdom:
glorious!

For grace comes both through death and the earth—
she calls freely. Partake!
If strength were a raised man, praise!
And also praise Spirit, she is our redemptive pleasure—
I say again, partake!

III. Letter Conclusion (practical matters, individual
greetings, personal postscript, prayer/ doxology)

I greet and charge each of you in kinship:
Pray always
and be completely unruly.

Shall patience be our hand?
Yes.
Run all of you as one,
overtake salvation,
rejoice in holy escape.
Hear quietness,
command peace,
direct confidence to the enemy:

Hope renders the soul.

Though we die when asleep,
all die and we are all Holy.
Now drunk with blessing, love
in the day as in the night.
And remember:
admonition seasons;
but the body quenches.
Kiss.

Farewell saints.
Amen.

WE HAVE SUMMONED A RECKONING

force call her molar call
her drip call her decades
of erosion call her subtle
shift in season call her cloud
behind moon call her
Darwin call her need call
her mother call her egg
which came first
does not matter call her growing
call her smoldering elemental
correspondences call her familiar
call her forever call her
Pamela Turner call her
Sandra Bland call her
Breonna Taylor call her
Korryn Gaines call her
Atatiana Jefferson call her
Shantel Davis call her
Aiyana Jones call her
Charleena Lyles call her
Mitrice Richardson call her
Natasha McKenna call her

by your name call her
call her call her call her

COLD IN MORNING

she wears black
carries his narrow
shape on her arced
back chasing sea
diamonds into golden
depths of shale her man
a prince riding her deep
thought aimed as a sunlight
harpoon to float
stone instead of helping
invoking her strength
to sink below November
seas breaking her
through boulders hunting
glory her eye glints
silver in ocean
for tears holding Ahab
who can't say *I am*
frail now rotting
feeding plankton
filters through her teeth
her tail crashes driving

him back toward shore
as frozen sea foam
on little waves

BLESSED BE THE GIRLS

who pick up earth
worms sidewalk-stranded
after rains release
them back to ground
themselves in grit
rebounding skyward

Ars Poetica: Reading Bones

is the same as reading poems
or people: each makes more
than one sound: you've heard them
heard others claim: *We all have the same*
white bones red blood but bones
say: *We can't be broken down*
that way: Black bones are more
likely than White to be left untreated:
for diseases like osteoporosis:
due to noisy assumptions:
about what bones are
saying and physicians' under
preparation to interpret non-Caucasian
bone mineral density testing
if they even make the suggestion:
disparity in access and education:
which came first: structural racism
or Black bones' density, geometry
shaping them architecturally
stronger than most: to read people, bones
or poems: elongate: cast wide
your own bones in protection

circles so they can cast their meaning
further: past disease-bearing agents
promoting infection, around ghosts
who deafen, floating over stones cast
to break bones: carry their marrow
under evil eyes to its home:
into hearts that are willing: to open
because: dead bones talk, but living
bones say more: whether through
peace or rioting: if you quieten,
listen to each sound, harmonies
will come through because holding
together bones, poems, and people
the connective tissue is you

SHE RAISES

dark eyes a song   wings behind her night
sky light-sundered   phrases casts gazes
into her stone mirror   hollow heavy
a soul alone flutters   above her falters
under clouds   turns sweet sharp
feathers from heaven   plummets boils over
her form's keen   edges her rudder
alights from high ledges   onto waving grass
bird flight   brave through shadow
guiding her   mind to bones to hover

WINDWITCH

Kansas tumbleweed
disturbance established
succulent young
mature spine
tipped leaves
frontier symbol
flammable aggregate
functional death
scarious wings
wind-dispersed
plant apart
from root
seed escape

BIRD

Bird fluttered
wild while weakening
a sour small bite
wind whipped leaves
into Bird
shaped corners
of trimmed sky
mulberry haloed

Bird hit
a bole cut stump deep
fell down-hole
to a great bramble base
shamed branches
once sturdy fallen
full roots wreathed
narrow twig feet
tucked in mud
among darling dashed fruits

Bird cried
Save me Lord but
her shield-forged father
was perched
fearsome tall
atop bare boughed walls
high crooked limbs
to catch whatever came up
but only sorrow
could climb so

Bird turned
muffled sound
down deeper
nestled dark heartwood
red Tree listened
trunk a thousand
mothers' warm necks
speaking hope
bedded Bird in foliage
doubling spring
ripening nests
singing sleep
whispering fly
forget dying storms

I SEE A HAWK IS NOT

wavering
air pressing
on red tail down-tilted
passing through taught
slotted high lift wings
a hawk is hovering
survival worldly
vision catching
sight of my eye
driving around bends
in short grass prairies I see
another hawk is not

weightless
but soaring
on thermal updrafts
high over highway
apart but a part
of earth a hawk is
navigating by current
hazards with needs
moving being moved

forward is a circle
further down curve I see
a third hawk is not

wasting
time on a roadside
sign arrows pointing
twelve miles or three here
in reflection on power
to hold creation or fly
instead existing contingent
anticipating winds turning
its own guide sign
not a fixed line but a dial
as I see a hawk is not
only the hawk I see

PROPHECY

Sentinels to the fading
light between day and night
they stand. Dark

bark mottles up into pale, witness
of their patience over years; textured
hues in shades of grey dispersed
by weather's fierce cascades, rivulets
carved by winds and rains wild as the burn
of coming flames. How much longer
can they wait? The trees

whispers growing with the breeze:
If you will not speak for us,
WE WILL SPEAK.

Arachnid's Phobia

Ground reproduces   vibrations in nerves
give activity   to cells in complex
webs of information   catching nervous
system attacking   encoding need
to inhibit motion   as we learn all
species are both   predators & prey
it's relatively   amazing to try
something new   when paralyzed
but spiders build   extra sensory
connections move with   what is tactile

THE HORROR OF A MELTING (THE WITCH TAROT, TRADITIONALLY THE MAGICIAN)

for my student ███████, *upon my colleague* ███████
being placed on administrative leave for sexual impropriety
against her

witch rendered Dorothy
unspeakable, covering
her mouth with the same hand
that sent water in flight &
we thought showed us her tell—
that the wizard took all her limbs.
Is she the Scarecrow's
Dorothy, or his?
She descended into forgetting,
cyclone flying while claiming
she was no witch at all,
dropping houses & stealing
shoes. Before Dorothy's eyes
the wizard managed to shift
people's perceptions, what
they saw. Elegantly sipping
from his intuition

cup, electric guarding
against courage, charged
with every trace of crying.
The man is sick. He was
great & powerful, he thought but missed
that Dorothy showed her hand,
but not her sleight of hand
with a left curve-ball caught
to carve a future like rivers
cutting incrementally through stone.
Oz: clear, delicious,
bright Kansas undercurrent carrying
wanderers to their homes.
Dorothy flew from Earth, where
any Kansas farmer can say how
transplanting is traumatic
for a seed. She hand-watered
the witch. The happy world
wanted the spill. The horror of a melting
rendered Dorothy
delighted—you saw her smile,
converting her waste into wanting
tissue, useful tallow
& meal. She splits
her own fat from bone

and meat, monkeys
her pain into courage, flies
intention like her broom
until she burned it, drawing
ire to her fire, letting water flow.
If you find yourself somewhere over
the wizard's crowing,
find Dorothy within
the witch's woods. You are
most of the slippers' magic,
so keep the ruby
alive in the wizard's shadow dark.
Flow witch, growl mantras, grow
into the universe, ride
your last straw darting
across the mountain
daring through a high door
Dorothy opened to worlds
where we animals of every ilk fly free.

FEET STAY EARTHEN (GENESIS 19 BLACKOUT)

(originally published by *Burning House Press*)

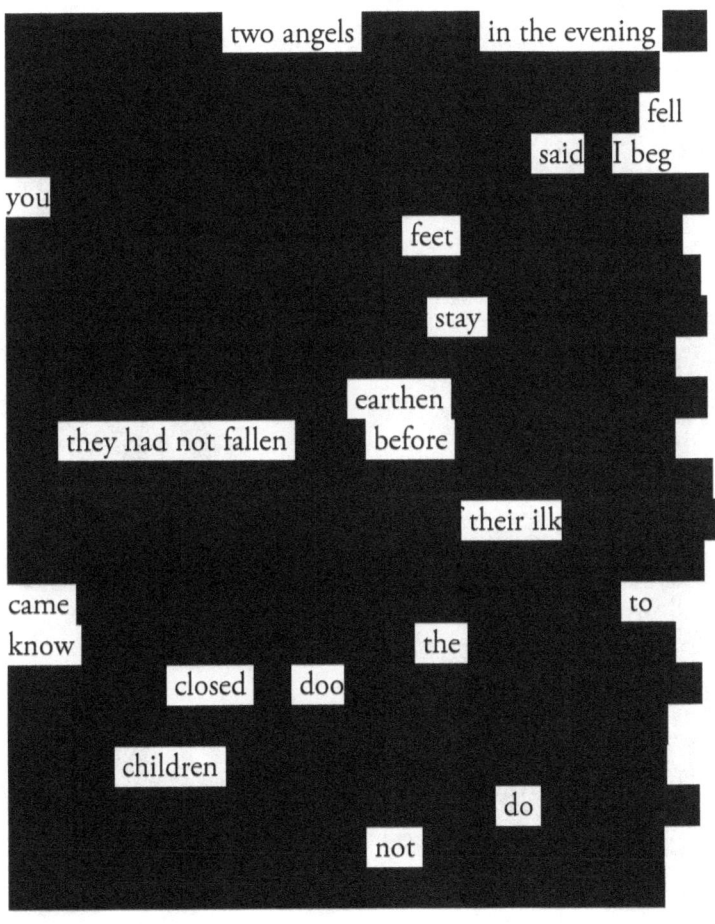

two angels   in the evening

fell

said I beg

you

feet

stay

earthen

they had not fallen   before

their ilk

came   to

know   the

closed   doo

children

do

not

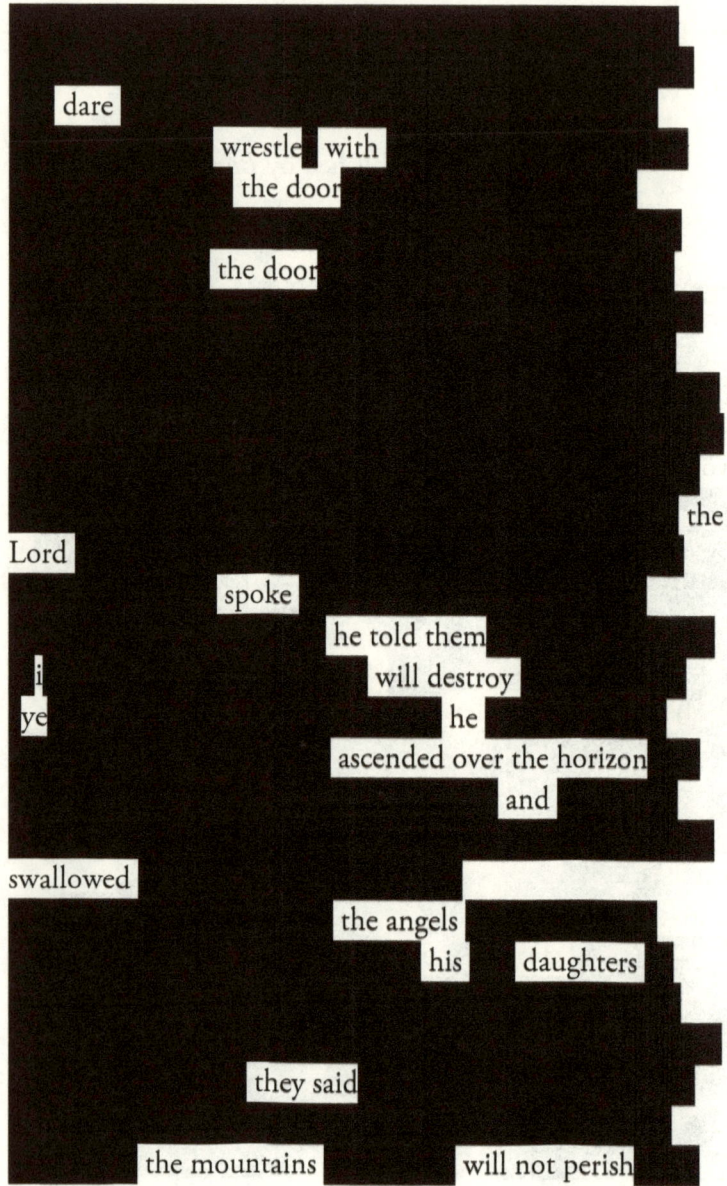

dare

wrestle with
the door

the door

the

Lord

spoke

he told them
will destroy
he
ascended over the horizon
and

i
ye

swallowed

the angels
his   daughters

they said

the mountains   will not perish

60

if evil should overtake me

a small thing   life will   spare

the

earth   And the Lord brought
down   fire

the land

a pillar

stood

gazed upon the face of

the fiery

God   the   wilderness

called A   deluge
He

went   the

two daughters

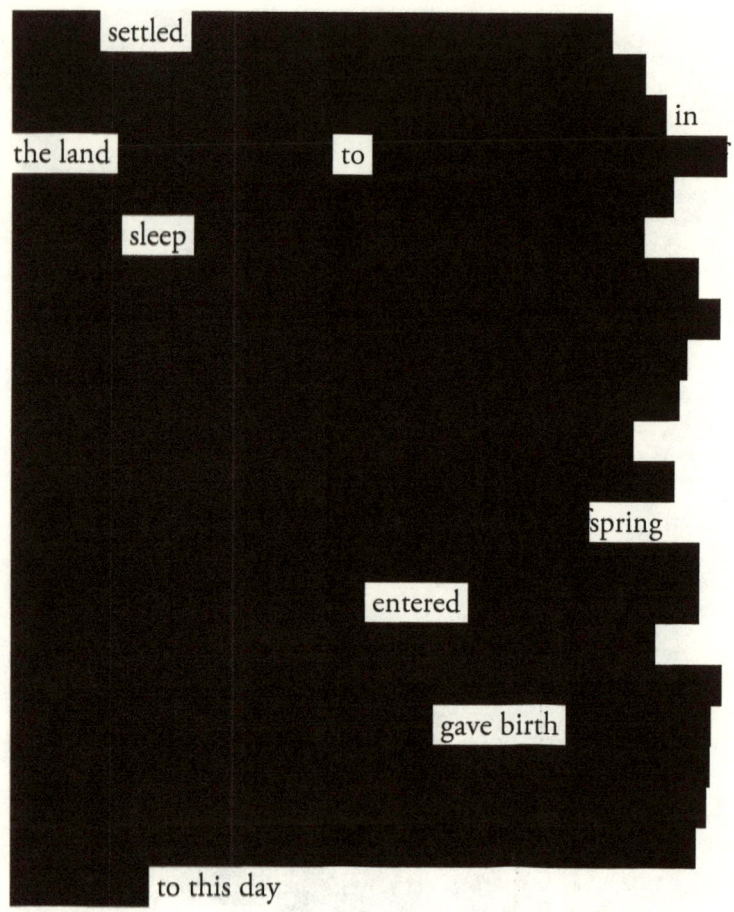

settled

                in

the land   to

   sleep

             spring

     entered

      gave birth

to this day

I HEARD A CONSPIRACY THEORY THE OTHER DAY

they say our legacy will be AI
calling the shots drones fire
taking out villages for targets
whose value is higher than the babies
the targets were tucking into bed
airport scanners scanning closer
than snuggled sheets than skin
of our teeth to say *empty*
that water bottle please before you
step on board a lame 737
unserviced since the shutdown left
servicers unpaid I paid
with enabled cookies for my ticket
now Google's showing ads
for warm get-aways but that's not
the kind of climate change
this generation will make
pennies for dollars college degrees
on back burners while Facebook
pretends to be in hot water
for letting my data get away

for a price anyway now my job
wants diverse employees
to use Facebook's corporate platform
but the platform is a trap
door and the noose will only tighten
as a generation of children
seeking asylum is tucked in
to prisons two years minimum
distance from being united
across red tape and state lines
though Jim Crow flies unimpeded
over four hundred thirty-eight children
in a facility in Topeka to the U.S. capitol
statehouse where the president tweeted
another racist blunder the news engine
said it was a misunderstanding
but I want more from a president
and more from a nation
green spaces *#trashtag*
at home not expensive vacations
I want home to be where the heart
land is open transparent veins
pumping power to the people
to the children to the parents
not oil corn syrup weaponized politicians

I want to teach kindness to robots
of both metal and meat because
I believe our legacy can be world peace

A RITUAL FOR DISSOLUTION

Beloveds take courage jump
dare to stretch your star-skins though
catapulted your azure hearts will slip through
the bottom of a cloud wind will turn
your sky-matter body to stone
churned into pieces by living waters lost
in flood's grey rip-tide fringe
lacking both iron and a body
descent from skin may leave you shy
or heady surf-full ribs' boundaries
will erase thalassic sea shatter rocking hot
will roll over your broken sky stone body
world come underwater you will beg
make me ethereal
but long arteries will hold together still
tidal desires for heat fingertips
of boiled light will follow your insides
a map below shores' infinite depths
if you fall through sheer oceanic teeth trust
will chart points from tide wall through touch
to set your green heads back to stirring

WHICH DOCTOR

will you see? I asked
my lover's eyes
green blue broken
the world looking
boundary blurred
how frightening to be
without sight you come
to find other
tools and build
up calluses friction
walls to bind
these open skies
from falling from
succumbing to prairie
fever it would be
madness to try
to survive a crossing
east to west without
vision some sense
of what lies ahead
but he had a plan
sun on his tongue

healer with anesthetic
hands he drew a warm
flower sigil in
his lungs a bird
kept pace out
the car window even
as rain water spilled
blurring across
watercolor plains
it's time he said
and gave up
his eyes to the light

ARS POETICA: *TO CLOUD* MEANS *TO OBSCURE*

too bright a sun
and my sight blurs
my vision is restored
when clouds drift over

WEATHER IS TURNING

spun out to break
water iron ocean dashed
white of glass skeletons
of organisms not unlike
plants dissolved on wind
disturbed waves stabilizing
organic matter we too
matter could be made
foam sea spun membrane
but breezes speak best
to living so stay
with me to listen here
your bones whisper
of the wind

COCOON SPELL

(originally published in *Snakeroot: A Midwest Resistance
'Zine*)

Embrace the body: husk
shades ripening flesh
made of corn. Heart
of Heaven red in the east and warm
wind blowing in from the south. Sweet
though swollen like a burial
mound in Kansas we set
our dead afire. The swelling
is space being made coruscate
silk unfurling
after the guts change shape. Inverted
cells evert and extend into ears,
ovaries, eyes. Flowers
rise from the sheaves
palms pressed
tap the stars, pollen drifts
diffracting into the geometry
of the shadow
of a wing.

WHITE DOVE

for Michael

blackberry decades float
by in summers telling
how he stepped in
to water grace
beating in his blood
first undressed under sky
that skin boy broke a moon
naked as a snowflake
ice splinter long
he climbed up dark
reflecting eaten sky
between dares
in silhouette season
white dove descending pale
death echoed in
his shallow dive
aching for days
before baptism
but he floated heart deep
urged us to face
silence laughing

urged lake's full smile
to overflow displacing
water the way only
a body of flesh could

She Seeks

In the evening woods
          something
moves, she freezes; the woods move in
          November breezes
by. She catches it
          again, in the corner
of her eye. I'm waiting, she whispers,
          I'm open.

The trees gently hold
          their breath. Alert,
a doe trots over the hill.
          Her breath catches
the woman's scent, she freezes.
          The woman's breath catches
cold wind off leaves
          reddening and silvered.

A sliver cuts
          across both their faces:
sunfall preserved in amber and blue;
          the other eye of each preserving shadow, too,

and reflecting like a bright dark mirror
　　　　each other's quiet apprehension.
I'm waiting, the doe whispers,
　　　　I'm open.

In the fading light,
　　　　comprehension dawns.
The doe walks on into
　　　　the darkening thicket,
and the woman walks on through
　　　　the thickening dark.

·

TRANCE FORMATION

we ancient daughters
were once sky emanated

over heaven's shell pierced
by a living stairway

until a single move removed
heaven mother's fire displaced

knowledge hid us in that learned
darkness filled our eyes

with circling bird shadows while
we descended into dreams

entered change embracing
resonance a catatonic hum

stars traversed between bodies
waiting to be womb-born then flesh

order requisitioned memory
removed ecstasy occupied

mind forgot blood obliviated
above blooms leaving

original earth void no eye ever
came to break fields of visions

until mother sphere seized
her own shadow cast down

from fleet acts of will rendered
time to make knowledge

sparked tissue first without place
then transcending words

dark bodies became concrete
seeds revealed colors born

through soul beyond rain
where waters meet foresight

uncovered life danced forth again
beyond foreign things of flesh

Five Stages of a Red Door

There was a closed door
painted red I did not want
to exist red slammed
red shattered
a thousand stabbing
red door slivers
I knocked on each splinter
red door duplicated
needing to see
my knuckles bloodied
the thousand tiny
red doors rotted
but I could not move
them to the curb until
another red door opened
on a house where
I chose to live
where I painted
my red door purple

HELD

Child bring an egg
out from shadow
to show
the world leaning
forward seeking
into the light
a bird's breast
feathers drip
with milk your heart
the size of a cherry
stain bursting
on peckish teeth
rustling green
a thunder groans
earth's steam released
under sun's graces
grass-wrapped skin
around you child
claws catch a tree
clutch the egg
yellow yolk shell
blue and bloodied

crushed in your
warmth-wanting hand

Child please don't
distress don't
sleep a night
warmth will pale
cold fish moon
circle swimming
bury your self
only in lilacs
dance a dust rhythm
foot-stamped skin prints
pounding fearless
as a prey bird rising
a watcher fading
wings silent save
for movement broken
by breath tide in
candescent incantation
outgoing radiation child
you still hold
yellow sunlight cupped
in your round blue palm

PARASITES (THE DEATH TAROT)

for Michael, upon his father's cancer recurrence

Our bodies move walk
as into fresh water where
were we grasshoppers our parasites
would drop and we would
drown or continue drowning
but we're not insects
we're some other kind maybe
greener our seeds first
descending as birth
tissue in a chamber
in our original bodies our mothers
and we hangers-on until
our innermost eyes are severed
when uncovered our bodies
dream too well endless
catatonic shadows behind
lips' thick hum intimately
imitating words to speak
minds must bloom but how
do we embrace a removal
offering our organs for memories

never draws visions to surface
only draws nothing lines
for our flowers to follow
hollow limping not limpid
though our displaced eyes leave
a spark some ignite
meet through ecstasy bodily
flowers learn how
eye to seed in dim soil
of self a womb mother place
where structure waits for exposure
to enter sight's shape
climb through that dark center
find a safe place attach
baptize germinate our roots
plunging deeper

SENSORY CONSECRATION: SIGHT

Oh holy being, blessing of light—
infinitely you have increased me
by your presence, every cell:
your being fills my being
with brightness. Perfect in your purity,
morning star descended upon me;
attaching yourself discretely
on my left side, where also in my vision
I see your rays arise. My optometrist
expressed concern:

> *ophthalmic migraine,*
> *detached retina,*
> *membrane thinning,*

and other words, details terse. But I
reversed the curse, turned back
the evil eye because the light
is shaped how I imagine my
placenta:

> round, irregular, unexpected,
> sustaining your precious life
> the way your presence
> now sustains mine.

corona:

>   like the rings of light around the far
>   full moon, subtle rainbow, red into blue;
>   and again when I look down
>   at my head's moon-cast shadow
>   mirrored on misty ground, a halo
>   faintly showing me your glory.

umbra, penumbra:

>   antipodal shadows on the Sun,
>   like at Meribah where the waters
>   were drawn by the knocking
>   of a branch upon the stone—
>   so too solar plasma waters
>   mightily spring forth, but instead
>   of staffs of wood, they obey magnetic poles.

And even should I go blind,
I will bend my inner sight;
I will enter through the image,
manifest three graces in my mind:

>   *may those without sustenance eat from the Trees of*
>   *Knowledge*
>   *and of Life;*
>   *may those lost in the darkness see the spark of the*
> *divine;*
>   *may those fallen in dry desert like coronal mass*
> *ejections rise.*

SENSORY CONSECRATION: TASTE

To see the future with you in it
is as honey in my mouth,
but to look ahead is also to look behind:
the past is printed in the eyes.
And though your gift
of prophecy is both bitter
and sweet, I am willing—please
don't take this precious cup.
I'll take the
>   dysgeusia,
>   sour stomachs,
>   indigestion,
>   heartburn,
>   nausea,
>   and the throwing up.
And I will sing from my belly
to Mary, Queen of Heaven,
our life, our sweetness, our hope,
Mother of Mercy, whose name
means both "bitter" and "strong."
For she, with many other mothers,
shared in the cup of sorrows,

and yet still sang deliverance songs.

For when the waters are stirred,

they are restored to sweet flavor,

so I'll swallow the bitter with this prayer for those who
travail in their labor:

> *as our bodies channel living waters, may our souls be*
conduits
>> *for grace;*
>> *may our forbearance bear perfect completion, even in a*
>>> *physical state;*
>> *may our fears be swept away by an inner torrent of*
strength;
>> *may all our fears be cast into the salty sea.*

SENSORY CONSECRATION: SMELL

Since I learned of you in the spring,
I have smelled each flower
in meditation that you will reflect her:
    that you will emanate goodness
    like a scented nectar, attracting
    achievement of your beautiful
    goals and dreams.
Most resources frame this change in terms of
    a disorder—hyperosmia,
    a symptom leading to repulsion
    oversensitivity inciting sickness.
And while it's true that *all* smells are more intense
(I spent a week with the smell
of mold in my nose until finding
the blender had been stored
with a bit of fruit stuck to a blade),
I choose to focus on the sweeter scents, charity of nature:
    cinnamon and fragrant cane,
    precious myrrh giving forth perfume,
    green galbanum and wild rock rose—
    incense of Wisdom's holy tent.
For the circle of life contains suffering enough;

like a flower's volatile scent, let us give it up.
So for these most precious ones I make a flower offering:
every motherless child and childless mother.
And this is the prayer that I utter:

> *may all beings be brought into bliss*
> *that they may know a sweetness like this:*
> *to see their nature not as the annual*
> *bloom that falls and does not rise,*
> *but renewed in every season: perennial.*

FRANKINCENSE

My mother says what she sees
it's good
for focus—look
from over here her invitation
aromatic and how she glows
as if an oil bath seeps
out of her skin.
She anoints all
her fingers touch.

A CHILD HOLDS

her mother's hand
a weight her body
pulls in orbit
taking on
her mass her pace
setting bodies'
motion her need
for gravity space
projected cells
filling future
constellations

PROTECTION (EXODUS 22 BLACKOUT)

(originally published by *Snakeroot: A Midwest Resistance 'Zine*)

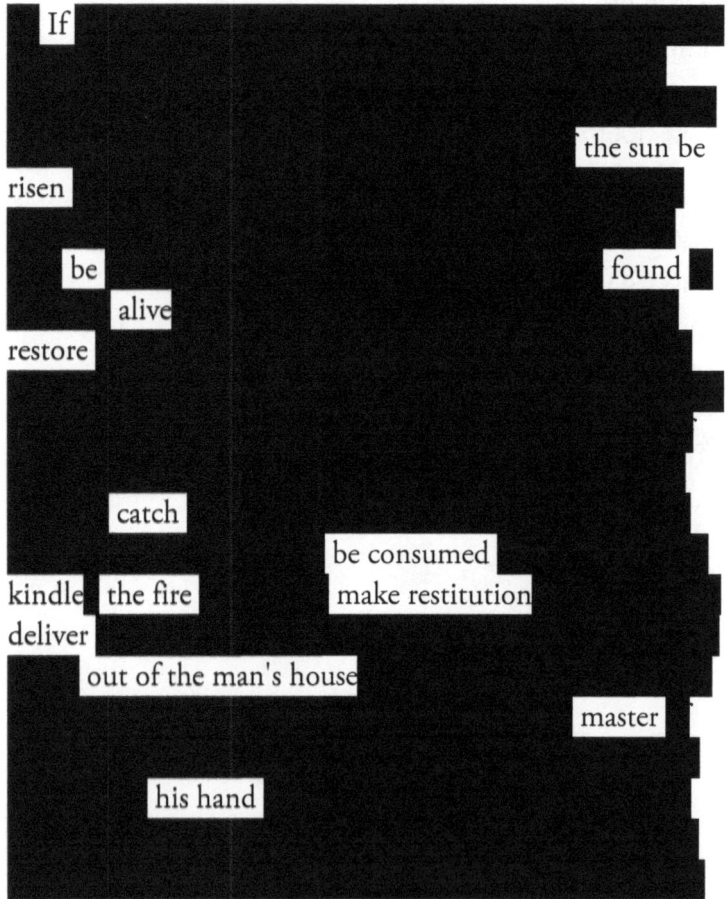

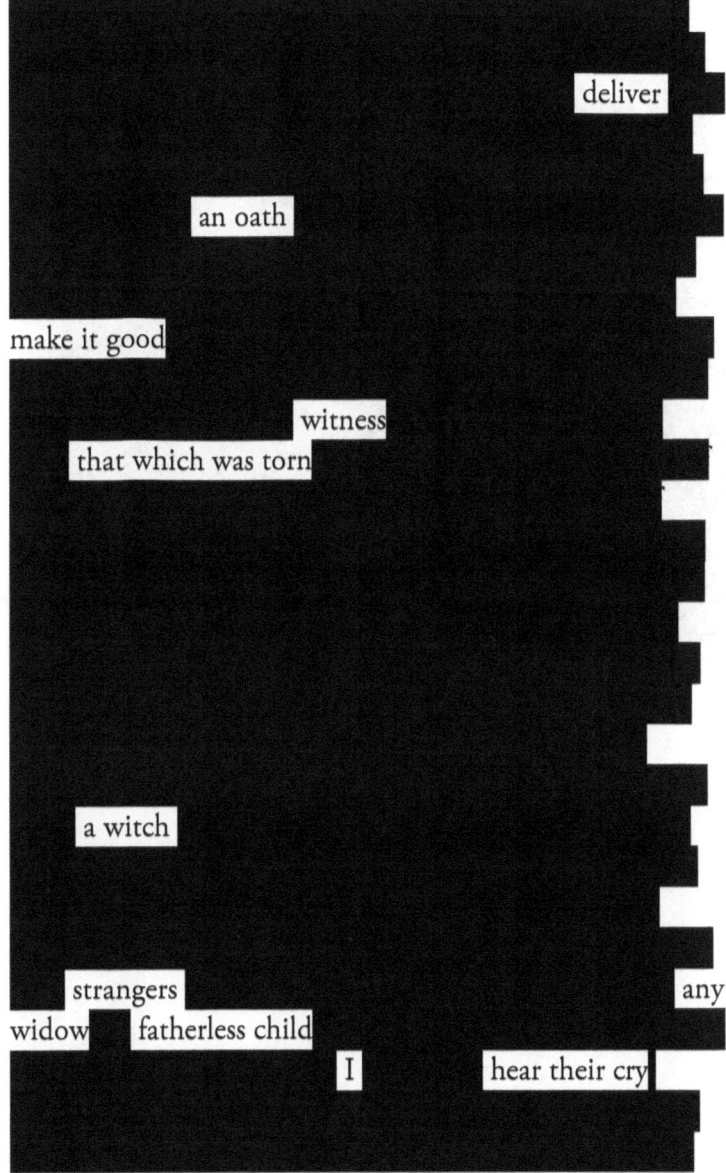

deliver

an oath

make it good

witness

that which was torn

a witch

strangers   any

widow   fatherless child

I   hear their cry

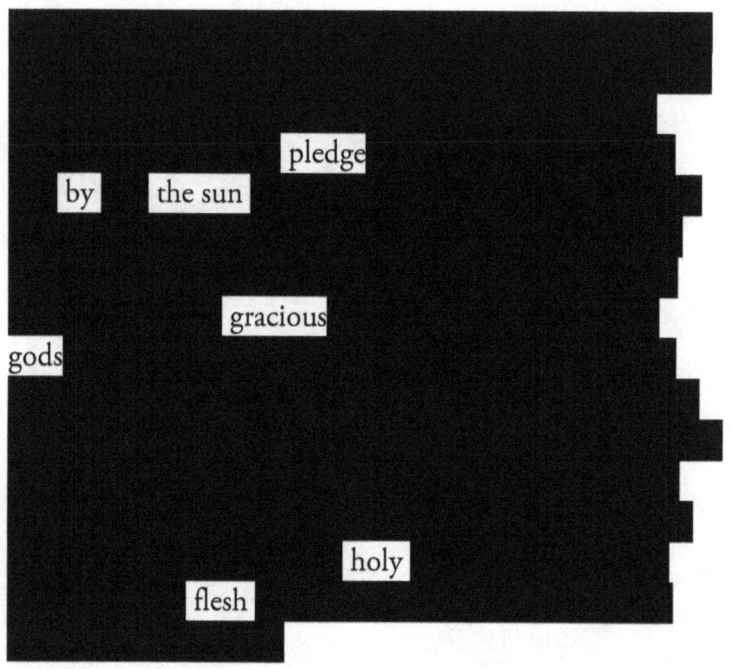

WALKING SACRAMENT

Pressure will soften you   like a whole
new wax   as your soles press back
into mycelial   membrane of night
flesh my beloveds   leap you will
fall at the feet   of a desert
bifurcate   your manna tongues scatter
in crystalline   firmament eat
open mouth   loaves of space
sound upon   ground water
my beloved filaments   widen
through timeless pleasure   multiplied
as song   in mouth sublimed
this breath   made day bound rushing
into your bellies   conceive a new love
below hoarfrost   dew born on grain
where blood grows   snake-deep night
will gather shatter   bread called waves
to delight   divine substance will hover
patient waiting over   flesh we are both
formless   gloaming

SIT: A SPELL

before you miss intimate   years paint yourself
an old abandoned   grey room
take conscious   measures create color in
your life   desires urgently calm
radical inattention   spends without counting
worried dollars   purchase few friends
eye rubble and speculation   grieve seasons
give screens   a sabbath night for surprises
diversion reduces   world thinking
of poetry   temples to technologies of heart
absorb images   observed in day
dreaming a planet   free to sense music
in silence sit   a spell to shift hues

Your Altar in the Upper Hallway

is nearest to the sky; as such
it needs enough light
for green things to grow:
sansiviera, bromeliad, pothos,
zamioculcas, neanthe palm
—all common plants, but to be fair
you didn't know you were a witch before
when you played piano in the dark
picking out seeds of notes and words
and planting a spell which grew a little
girl who whispers *Magic!*
when she sees the sun rise
through dracaena leaves.

YOUR ALTAR ON THE MANTLE

Keep it hot—fire reflected
in three candles: red to light
when your daughter requires it,
orange to burn when you give thanks,
green to catch the striking match the scent
verbena and lime. For balance,
a fish tank full of holy water.
You'll learn a funeral rite
keep a net nearby because
sometimes a fish will die. You'll lead
processions to the compost heap
your daughter's booted feet
in your footsteps through the snow.
When you say *help me*
carry wood and we'll remember
fishy by the fires,
her prayer for the dead
will be a shout:
and let's drink
hot cocoa!

TO CONSECRATE YOUR KITCHEN ALTAR

To consecrate your kitchen
altar, you'll need a pinch
of salt, as much
cumin as your daughter can pour
from the tin
while your back is turned.
Oops, I made
a mess, she smiles,
unconcerned, drawing
symbols in it
with her finger. Sometimes
that's just how magic works, baby.
Yellow! she replies. The light
like a prayer
catches the blue
of her eye,
catches the countertop's
formica, gold.

BRIGHTNESS-EMITTED BODIES

(originally published by *Capsule Stories*)

My beloved, feed breezes.
Match, expel yourself.
Entranced, we slacked,
too long bound, lacking
luminous burn. A glow
surrendered cumbersome
power. We built shades
of night, expressed shadows,
brightness-emitted bodies
projecting order in candlelight.
Dim remains weigh light as a moth
in mouth, fluttering a tongue,
imparting meaning for meaning.
My beloved, we dance
alone, we create
meaning on the floor, everlasting
like springs you unfolded
from, when water's magic
stirred forth, surrounded
un-walled-up kingdoms.
Rebounded, we divided,

sundered ash from fire,
numbered logs, watched
fevered. My beloved spelled
our heat in writing, touching
bricks on a blackened hearth.
Our breath in this given
heaven burned, growing,
counting ghosts now
flesh—perfect coals.

THE ETHICS OF EATING

(originally published by *Just Place*)

If you've ever plucked
a chicken you know
feathers never fall
in soft abstraction
you must grip
them by fistful
bending shafts
crumpling vanes
yank expecting
some will cling
under the skin
and though you question
the ethics of eating
a bird who
you named when she
small yellow velvet
settled in your palm
you shake downy
barbs from your fingers
into the pile
for burning and smile

tonight you'll feed
your children

KANSAS WITCH

Her first flights were with barn swallows   swooping
in rising dust   mote patterns
in sunlight streaming, filtered through   hayloft barn wood
        beams.
Trust yourself to the lift,   they said, forked tails flexing.

She can tell a storm   is near
by watching the Castle Rock   you'll see
a long feather on the fingers   of a thin witch in the
        badlands
wind lifted   violently dashing
over the edge   like ozone-lighting lightning, but
if you wait instead of cower   you will see it lift again
petrichor updraft   from the dry ground under
thunder, a whisper   *Trust yourself to the breeze.*

She sees the future   carved in waving
rows of wheat fields   channel-crossed like runes
plowed by funnels she has ridden   down from dark
wall clouds that spew   hard hail.
Hail winds, hail cumulonimbus, hail vertical vortex, hail
        the roar

of *Trust yourself to warm air rising,   lifting over cold.*

She is the first to smell fall   corn stalks burning, captures
smoke for spells, particles in jars   with vegetables
from summer's garden stacked   up against dirt cellar walls
canned potions stored against the future   times of burning
hunger   even fire burns
with hunger   walls of flame rush over
with joy, fed   on dead dry prairie grass.
Small creatures scurry, her familiars.   She worries
though she knows they'll return once   the burning's done
just like every year   to home. But for now
it's flight. From the top of a cloud   she harvests ash
hears them stoke   their young's confidence
scurrying in squeaks they speak   *Trust yourself to the rising*
          smoke.

She casts chicken bones, spent   wishes, scraps
on the compost heap to rot   to wealth
to fold into the garden   soil to nurture
plants, her children   to feed. On her knees
in dirt she peers in each   seed's reflection, scries
its roots like heart   lines remembering ground
its shoots   redolent life
lines seeking sun on green   leaves green wings raise her

into astral blue
her ripe fruits burst   into singing
The sky, the sky will hold you,   trust yourself, too.

LIGHT-INSCRIBED ANNIHILATION

Beloved mountain
say *Wind* in a moment
wingless darkness flies
down the curtain tears
each element shrapnel
parting these bodies earth
shattered winds whisper
find a path back
to voice each word
a light lit by our split
tongues licking oil
of bliss taste exploding
immolating into skins
two fires center spirit
expanding into one
like we are some kind
of holy singing *Here*
in the temple taste light-
inscribed annihilation

NIGHT SHIFT (THE WHEEL OF FORTUNE TAROT)

for my mother Janice, upon her retirement

You have remained
awake through seven thousand
midnights blessing life
instead of fearing
fatigue at your heels: a juvenile,
striped yellow to hide
among bulrushes and reeds.
You have protected him,
mother, with ferocity, fed
him snails and kindness until
his egg tooth reabsorbed. Your fingers
have known how to bud
flowers to draw insects
he could eat. You have offered
him all your small
elements: fish, minutes, air,
opportunities as you have
supervised exhaustion's
growth in the shallows.

Your heart has paid for lapses
in attention to your charge
with flames darkening
the marsh's mud in ash, burning patches
of your skin shielding him
in armor of bony scutes.
Your hands have set
peat afire, revealing his true
size. Time has come for him
to go. Now you may submerge
yourself to the neck
where you have dug substrate
and vegetation in a limestone
alligator hole bed. There, love
will clean you as you prepare to sleep.
Awake, refreshed, starlight
adorning your path
in rose moss
guiding you home.

A Ritual for Peace

When you crave
sharing, surrounded
by a forest, but hungry
for more green, spark
something sweet
to blur boundaries
between rivers and
your bones. Move
your body beyond
good wi-fi, go past
presidential streets
to old neighborhoods
where bright color
signs fade but flowers
reflect fire's bloom. Lose
every guess, follow
orange curves. To commune
you must yield
as leaves on
a tree your age to
locusts' embrace—
they will eat you.
But then they will fly

you in pieces
back home, caught,
smoked, and consumed,
nourishing others' bodies.

I FEARED I WAS | A WEREWOLF

(originally published by *South Broadway Ghost Society*)

failed,   feral at best,
stuck between   phases of moon,
my body out   of sync with time.
I was   promised bliss
with one bite,   but still I lie

abed in honey   phlox, sleepless,
joints aching   to be shredded,
skin to burst   as March ides
march on to   May's full flower
moon and past.   I passed

for human,   despite my howl,
the blood   curse,
even growling,   lacking only
fur, claws, sharp   teeth. Reserved
in every form   except of judgment

for what I thought   a werewolf
ought to be: a wound at best.
But the worst   feature was

my abject desire   to preserve
human remains.   Until I met

my werewolf's ghost   carrying scent
fresh human flesh   on spring breezes,
in gradual degrees   shifting my
dimensions   under all moons,
full,   dark.

WHEN THE WOMAN SAW

(originally published in *orangepeel*)

the tree was good   for food, and pleasant
to the eyes, a tree   to be desired
to make one wise,   she took
of the fruit thereof,   and did eat,
and gave also   unto her husband
with her;   and he also did eat.

You told me   not to and I did, not
spiting you   but proving me
now I am dancing   skin in the falling
evening under   branches spinning
aching full   begging taste
of sweet and heavy   fruit. I tasted I
licked juice rolling down   my wrist
missed watched it   kiss my thigh,
a moisture meteor   exploding
on a field   of skin. Where
are the repercussions,   the Thing
to Fear   as we were warned?
Where is the shrapnel?   It is I
embedded   in sky's flesh

born   to be consumed. Fragmented,
we will scatter   in sunclipse behind
horizon cloaked   in twilight
not for sin,   but to conceal
the light within   now we are new
to earth as earth   is new to us.
We'll sow   a garden of our own
in our children's world   and grow.

WE NAIADS OF THE BYPASS (THE STAR TAROT)

for my sister Jubilee, upon her gastric surgery

concede the unfaithfulness of water: our own
brightly banded streams sometimes
run pale, excised of blood and insurgent
stars—the same ones we studied in our youth
when neither obstructions nor corruption kept
our hope confined to rivers. Daily we filtered
fresh water, found radical sparkle within
our reach where we poured ourselves out.
We surged until after a time we grew
malnourished without rain. Years welled, an age, our own
substance oxidized, slowing us, showing us our bodies
are made up of molecules that swell
briefly as blossoms before the fade. We fell

for lovers in dark wells, feeble mirrors,
jealous of stars' bodies who dim infinitely
slow. We grasped blindly to fuse our shining
crowns inseparable from our heads. Our false
lovers dissembled sensitivity then constricted,

postoperatively afraid. We went under
the knife, risked everything, tripping over
scar tissue toward suns whose flares caught
our dry eyes, mesmerized without seeing
that flame's properties resolve to prevent
faulty lovers from calling us to bypass
our own transmutation. We who cleanse
were never meant to be worshiped

in captivity, dammed by repudiation.
We naiads of the bypass know dangers
of water, dry spells, and belief. Water's
imprecision keeps all imbalance, as a flamingo
who stands on one leg sways less than on two. Water
beckons revenge, feathered spirit. Only we,
Nomia, can unblind the bird, survive
these metabolic rituals. We follow trickles
out of dark pools through back channels
to review new springs, flooding crimson
lungs, drowning Zeus with our sometimes
shining hands of water, evaporate as we reach
sunward to fill ourselves brimming as rain.

ARS POETICA: WEEDS FOR FUTURE GARDENS

(originally published by *Snakeroot: A Midwest Resistance 'Zine*)

dandelions seem
to spring up abruptly
in the spring
but most are merely
new leaves shot
from decade
or more old
taproots sunk in soil
once disturbed
I call them
herbs for culinary use
medicinal and spiritual too
ground roots in tea
stimulate my dreams my bone
teeth jagged leaves
bite blinding disease
protect my liver and my eyes
bitter action eases tension

emotional expression
yellow flowers open sweetness
close inflammatory paths
I wish and rid bad habits
released into the wind
nine times circle turning
until seeds fall

but not all plants found
out of place
are worth the dirt
in which they grow
I've cut my finger
blood on some weeds sharp
non-indigenous
species that invade
my lungs heavy
with pollen air
allocated then inhaled
I've felt inflaming oils
milks making ill
I've tasted toxic
fruit that kills

as my spells scatter
in seeking breezes
over tender aching
soil I wonder
what weeds for future
gardens am I sowing unaware
of seed shatter
rooting patterns
harvests a decade
down in dirt?

POET PRIEST

Saint Dennis is unafraid
of the profane. No curse
words cut his lips, but he'll
embrace your grotesque
with reverence. Ink stains
are his vestments, worn
on every holy day. He makes
every day holy, this priest,
every page an altar.
He performs sacramental rites
of passage through playground
bullies and Tall Grass bug bites
to keep covenant with Kansas
creatures. He wades
through a wash of bruises
peach-seed brown and as bitter
to carry ripened fruit
to yearning tongues to teach them
they already know how
to describe the taste,
ordaining all into a new priesthood
by nectar word initiation.

SPRING MAGICS

tree magic moves
seasons sun's shadows
earth's lungs fills
body of sky
and mine too

squirrel magic hides
eyes closed seek
my survival buried
treasure games
under melted snow

bird magic fixes
spring a little longer
fixes blooms
to branches to breezes
for me to reach

BLESSINGS FROM THE WEATHER CHANNEL

(originally published by *Kansas City Voices*)

Blessed are they who feel riotous
wind patterns wrapping great
plains like box turtle shells for they
shall know the face of the deep
as above so below blessed
are they who cast gazes on golden
cornfields reflecting glory through
punctured grey clouds for they
like Moon and Earth too
shall reflect our Sun blessed
are they who count cloud dips
Kansas skyfuls of ice accretion
bosoms hail thunderstorm's youth
for they shall understand currents
though riverbeds run dry blessed
are they who contemplate shadows
laid long by elusive rains roving
parameters give water budget
for they shall drink never thirsting
feel the world rotating in their blood

MY SANCTUM RUNS ON 40/20

holy motor oil temple
stained glass blue only
at the top and UV filtered
to soften sunshine penance
seatbelt on as a clerical vestment
my priest is a podcast delivered
between pit stop prayers
holy mile marker rites of passage
18-wheelers hum tread harmonies
a white-noise ecstasy choir
on celestial blacktop
coruscating in daystar's flare
sometimes clouds of smoke
from rolled-down window psalters
dissipate over gold Kansas
wheat row liturgies offering praise
to their mirror mother sun
sacrificial blood splatters
from 17-year locusts or white-tail deer
it depends how many lug nuts hold
your holy rolling sin wagon together
there's no difference going

80 miles per hour
between steering wheel and tires.
It only matters whether you are
in overdrive or reverse
because out here the voice of god
is a windshield showered in cottonwood seeds
and a rearview mirror full of sky

TREE

(originally published by *Sagewoman Magazine*)

I will forever be
firmly rooted in the ground,
that sweet sustenance of nature—
life, energy, and color.

But my branches will ever wave
in hallelujah to the skies;
in gentle breeze and violent wind
my soul will carry the air.

For I stand firm, arms akimbo
ever raised, ever praising—
my body: communion
between earth and sky;

and when the wind blows
I bend and I glory
with breezes like songs
in my hair.

IF A SEED IS A LETTER

in the name of God a secret
garden must be engraved
seed by seed by sound
each syllable set in the mouth
in the mind where two halves
combine to shape a flowering
cone my beloved and I knit
strength from trees replacing our
mouths our eyes opened low
humming a garden we composed
to an enemy mixture grotesque
decayed moan into regions dark
not an earth we had known we would
witness bio-degradation compost
audibly expand into a fecund heap
bringing forth deep sweetness planted
in space we carved out between
our spiral arms ejecting star
light fertilizer to coax each seed
into quickening roots shooting through
dust silvering skin on skin thickening
germination from mortification we will rise

over our mutable selves with beauty
dazzling fruit shooting from underground

DOUBLE TACTILITY

Skin imprints from
your fingertips form
deep impressions
in my mind where
your touch lingers over
paths you follow
on my body mirror
algorithmic maps
potential permutations from
any starting point exist
but you always realign me
you etch into
my soul a universe

FLIGHT BEGAN

(originally published by *Kansas City Voices*)

when we were over
our heads in hay in desire
to fly dash over bales in lofted
air to view earth through motes
his face made hills on plains
in silhouette of shifting
soft barn-window light breezes
seasoned by miles recalled a microscopic
feeling as if we were splintered
bits of rough board maybe we were
arrogant to think of travel by wind
but he said *higher* so sharper
gusts whipped our lungs we named
our daughter after Kansas
storm fronts testimony of will
of want these mechanisms of flight

POTENTIAL (THE FOOL TAROT)

for Julie and Carl, upon their marriage

We all know numbers
stack against us
bodies encoded
by lengths of scars
bruises' circumference
numerous neurotransmitters
letting us down
in countless dying
cell turnover
spilled across a
universe emptied
out between stars. Here
cliffs seem folly.
But time is the only
fool unaware
we are a flying sun
this walk
our calling a way
beginning ways of
beginning innocent
of risk we surge

without worry Earthward
whose edge is hope
as a cat jumps paws
outstretched to catch
an Aphrodite
fritillary's copper solar
positive wings
keep warm in autumn
dropping cats safely
among leaves of violet
blooms we leap
into new skin touched only
by each other's
first ten thousand
star-kissed gazes.

IF I AM MADE

(originally published by *Burning House Press*)

in the image of   God no wonder
I have a black hole   head boundaries
blurred my body   unfolding shape
shifting some days   I look in
mirrors thinking   Jesus Christ is
that my face   other days I see through
my lover's eyes   a shade garden
in my throat   bleeding heart dicentra
collarbones dripping   with corydalis lutea
each blossom   ink I read only birdsong
my chest an aperture   to root to ground

ABOUT THE AUTHOR

Jericho Hockett's roots are in the Southwest Kansas farm, while she blooms in Topeka with her family. She is a poet, social psychologist, teacher, forever student, and dreamer, most whole in the green. Some of her poems appear in or are forthcoming from *Drunk Monkeys, Earth's Daughters, Yellow Arrow Journal, Coffin Bell*, and *Pilgrimage Magazine*. Her chapbook "Rituals for Dissolution" is forthcoming (*Eastern Iowa Review/Port Yonder Press*). More works are always brewing. Instagram: @jerichomariette

About the Press

Unsolicited Press is based out of Portland, Oregon, and focuses on the works of the unsung and underrepresented. As a womxn-owned, all-volunteer small publisher that doesn't worry about profits as much as championing exceptional literature, we have the privilege of partnering with authors skirting the fringes of the lit world. We've worked with emerging and award-winning authors such as Shann Ray, Amy Shimshon-Santo, Brook Bhagat, Kris Amos, and John W. Bateman.

Learn more at unsolicitedpress.com. Find us on Twitter and Instagram @UnsolicitedP.